HOW WWI CHANGED MODERN WARFARE

HISTORY WAR BOOKS

CHILDREN'S MILITARY BOOKS

BABY PROFESSOR

EDUCATION KIDS

Speedy Publishing LLC

40 E. Main St. #1156

Newark, DE 19711

www.speedypublishing.com

Copyright 2017

In this book, we're going to talk about how World War I changed modern warfare. So, let's get right to it!

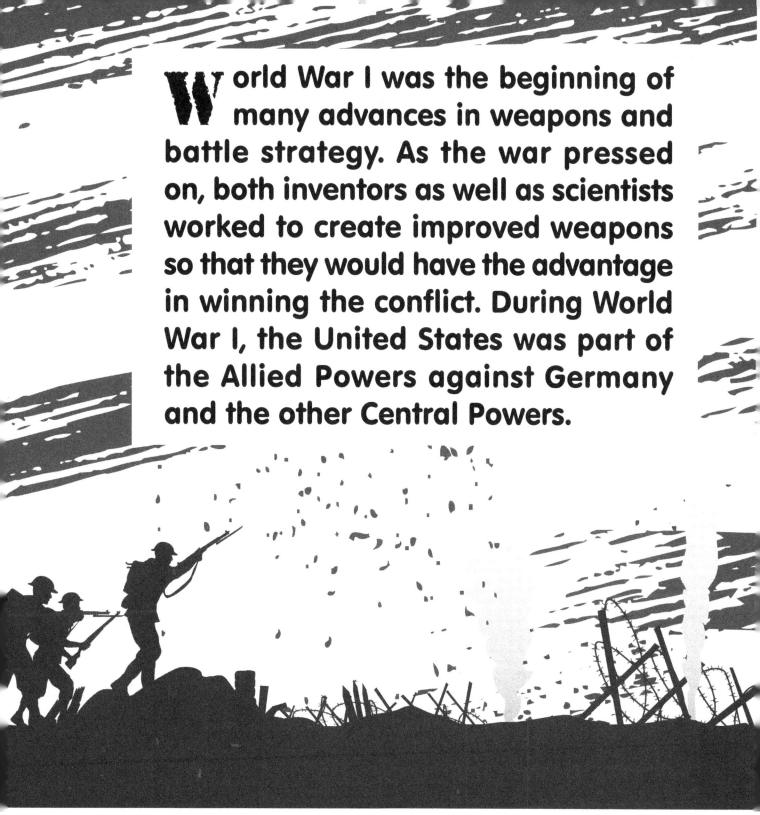

World War I was the beginning of many advances in weapons and battle strategy. As the war pressed on, both inventors as well as scientists worked to create improved weapons so that they would have the advantage in winning the conflict. During World War I, the United States was part of the Allied Powers against Germany and the other Central Powers.

AIRPLANES FOR SPYING AND BOMBING

When World War I broke out in 1914, airplanes had only been around for a decade. Aircraft played a minor part in the conflict at the start, but, by the war's end, the air force had emerged as a very important division of the armed forces. The very first aircraft used for military purposes were sent aloft to view the pathways of enemy troops and send back valuable intelligence information.

AIRCRAFT

At the beginning, if enemy planes came close in the air, the pilots would acknowledge each other's presence but that's all they would do. At that point, they didn't have any weapons, but this soon changed. Some daring pilots began to shoot pistols or throw grenades at the

enemies. Before long, machine guns as well as cannons were mounted on the aircraft's wings or nose. This was the beginning of the first fighter planes.

WWI TWO-SEAT BIPLANE DAY BOMBER

RECONNAISSANCE

At the start of the war, fighter planes like the French-made Morane-Saulnier Type N shot down enemy bomber planes and reconnaissance aircraft. Reconnaissance aircraft were planes that were gathering military intelligence about the enemy's troop movements and locations. These types of attacks thwarted the enemy's progress, but they weren't really battles in the air.

MORANE-SAULNIER PLANE

RECONNAISSANCE AIRCRAFT

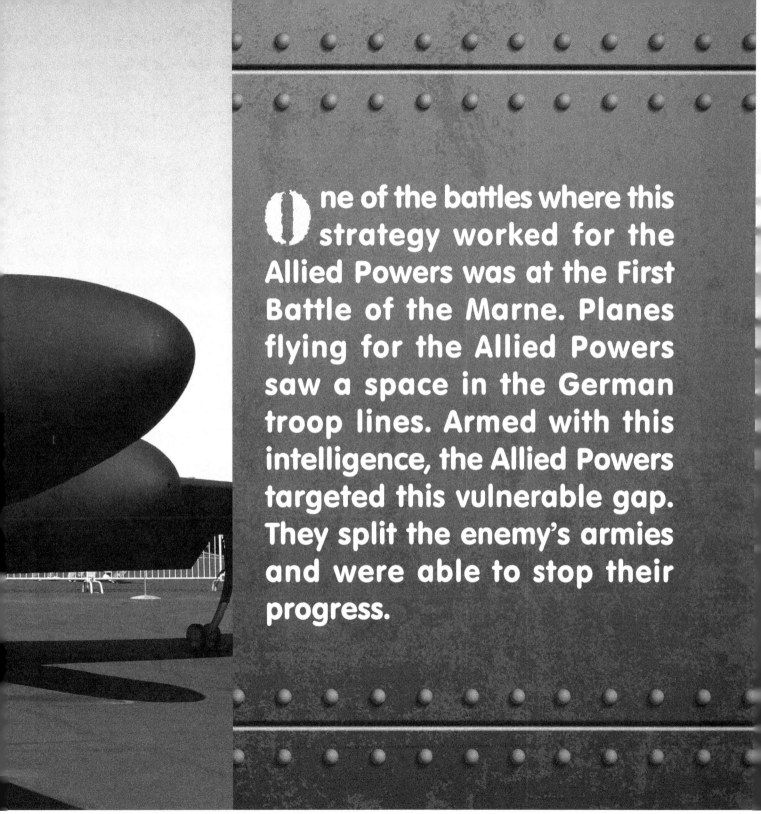

One of the battles where this strategy worked for the Allied Powers was at the First Battle of the Marne. Planes flying for the Allied Powers saw a space in the German troop lines. Armed with this intelligence, the Allied Powers targeted this vulnerable gap. They split the enemy's armies and were able to stop their progress.

BOMBINGS

As the war went on, the Allied Powers and the Central Powers started to use airplanes to throw bombs down on important enemy locations. The first bomber planes could only transport small bombs. They could easily be attacked from shots fired at ground level. However, by the war's end, heavy-duty bombers with a much longer flying range had been built. These bombers could carry and drop much heavier bombs.

HEAVY BOMBER

WARNING
OPERATE INERTIAL SEPARATOR
BEFORE COWLING REMOVAL

PROPELLER PLANE

DOGFIGHTS

As more planes were filling the skies, pilots began to fight each other by shooting with rifles or pistols. It was very difficult to shoot down an enemy plane this way. Soon, mounted machine guns were used. However, there was a major problem. With a machine gun in the front of the plane, the airplane's propeller was in the wrong position as the machine gun was fired. The shots damaged the propeller and didn't get to the target enemy planes.

The Germans invented a type of machine gun that would work in the same cycle as the propeller. This invention, called an "interrupter," was soon part of the standard fighter plane equipment on both sides of the conflict.

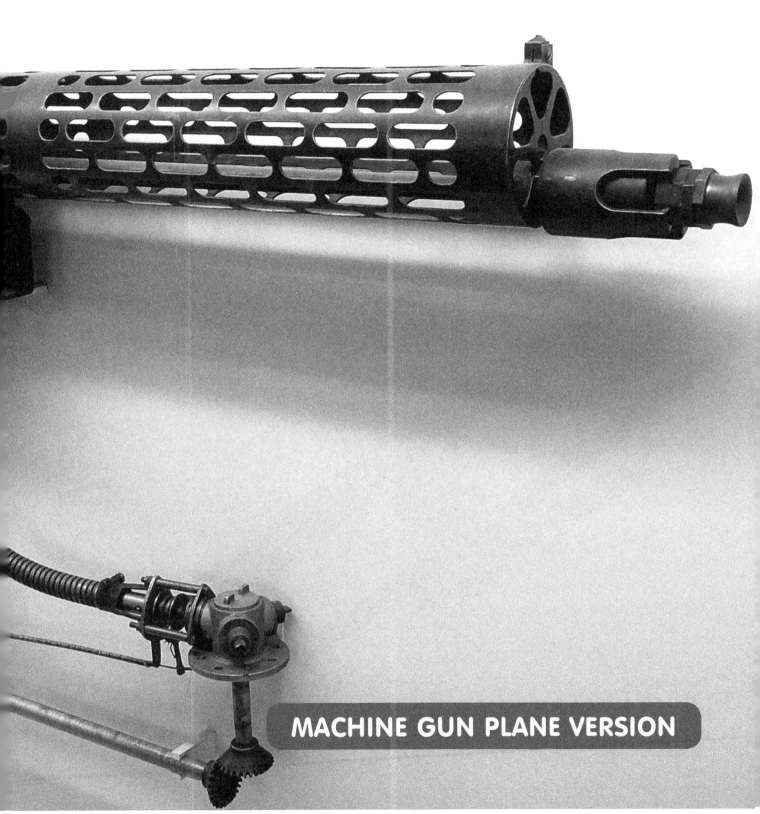

MACHINE GUN PLANE VERSION

ow that pilots could shoot at each other with machine guns, the World War I era of dogfights began. The term "dogfight" had been used for centuries for very fierce battles that were fast paced. These battles in the air were daredevil fights to the death as one enemy shot down another in close range in the sky. The best pilots, those who flew the most successfully and shot down many enemies, were called aces.

These aces kept track of every plane they destroyed. They became decorated for their bravery and were famous when the war was over. The top fighter pilot for the Allied Powers was the Frenchman Rene Fonck. He shot down 75 enemy planes and amazingly survived the war.

RENE FONCK

MANFRED VON RICHTHOFEN

The top fighter pilot for the Central Powers was the German Manfred von Richthofen. He shot down 80 enemy planes before he was shot down and killed by a British pilot.

He was given the nickname the Red Baron because he flew a plane that was painted red.

WORLD WAR I AIRPLANE MARKINGS

From the ground, it was difficult to tell whether a plane was flying for the Allied Powers or the Central Powers. Often, ground troops would shoot down a plane only to find out that it was from a country that was on their side. To avoid this, countries began to mark their planes with clear symbols so that others would know what side they were on. At that time, planes flew much more slowly than they do today. Their top speed was about 100 miles per hour, so the symbols painted on them could be seen from the ground.

AIRCRAFT CARRIER

One of the major problems with aircraft for war maneuvers was that they were limited in their range by the amount of fuel they could carry. Toward the end of the war, the aircraft carrier was invented. These were ships designed so that airplanes could take off and land on them.

AIRCRAFT CARRIER

MODERN AIR TRAFFIC CONTROL TOWER

AIR TRAFFIC CONTROL

At the start, once a pilot left the ground, he was out of contact and unable to get information except for lamps or flags that were signaled. The year 1917 was the first time that a human voice was sent by radio waves to a plane in flight thanks to innovations by the United States army.

TRENCH WARFARE

For many centuries, battles had been fought on the ground and soldiers used trenches. Armies in World War I made extensive use of trenches. The land between the Allied Powers and Central Powers trenches was called "No Man's Land." Trench warfare was a slow and deadly way to fight.

TRENCH

WOOD STOCKED BOLT ACTION RIFLE WITH A HIGH POWERED SCOPE

Millions of troops died on both sides, but little ground was gained. One of the weapons used by the British during trench warfare was the bolt-action rifle.

TANKS

Tanks were a new innovation during the war. At the beginning, they were thought of as landships, but soon got the name tanks because they resembled metal water tanks. The first prototype of what would become the tank was called the British Mark I, which went by the code name "Little Willie." Tanks were first used by the British to cross the "No Man's Land" area between the trenches in order to attack the Germans.

MILITARY TANK

The tanks had thick outside armor to protect them against enemy fire. The crew of each tank had a driver as well as a commander and a gunner. The gunner's job was to fire the cannon and machine guns that were on board.

NAVAL WARFARE

In addition to the inventions in the air and on land, there were changes in naval warfare during World War I as well. Huge battleships named dreadnoughts traveled the seas. These enormous ships had outsides with an armor made of metal to fend off enemy fire. They carried guns that fired long distances so they could hit targets both on land and sea.

THE LAST WORLD WAR ONE DREADNOUGHT BATTLESHIP

THE BATTLE OF JUTLAND

The Battle of Jutland was one of the main battles fought by sea. Ships belonging to the Allied Powers created a blockade so that Germany would not receive their needed supplies or food.

At the beginning of World War I, the British Navy had the largest fleet of submarines. It took a while, but soon the Germans had submarines as well. The Allied Powers called the German submarines, U-boats to distinguish them from the Allied submarines.

MILITARY SUBMARINE

LUSITANIA

Torpedoes fired from submarines and U-boats at close range caused destruction of both ships and other submarines. At the beginning of the war, it was Germany's attacks on passenger ships such as the Lusitania that propelled the United States to join the war effort.

NEW OR MODIFIED WEAPONS

Many weapons were invented or improved during World War I.

MACHINE GUNS

Machine guns were very difficult to move because they were so heavy. During World War I, new models were created that were much lighter in weight and easier for soldiers to carry.

MACHINE GUNS

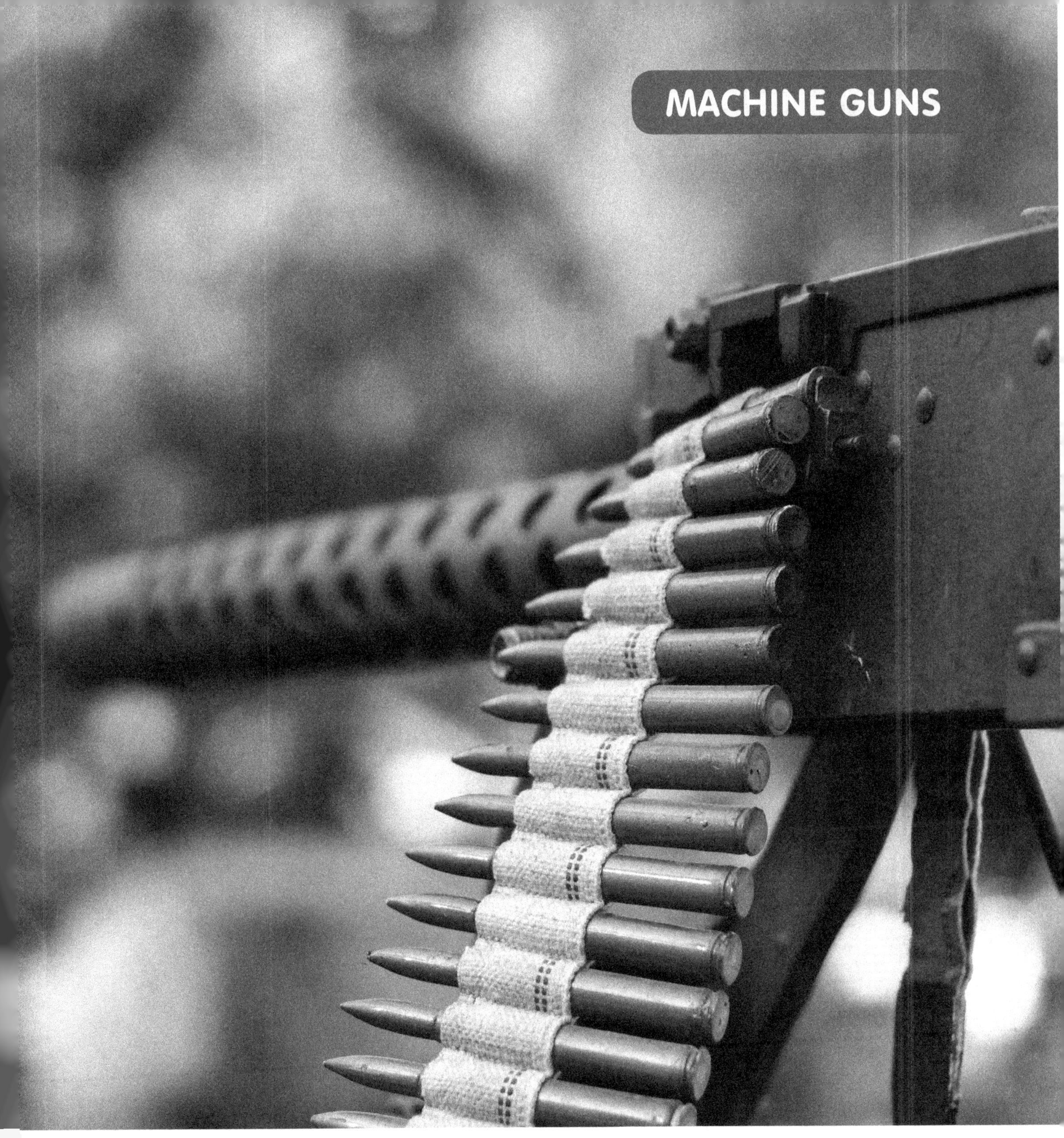

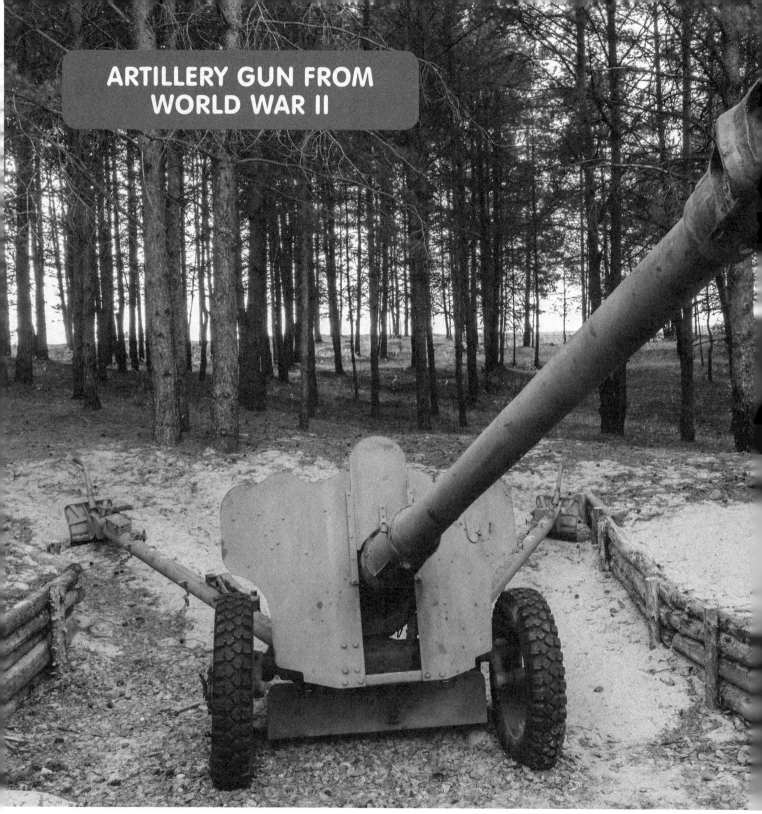

ARTILLERY GUN FROM
WORLD WAR II

ARTILLERY

Artillery guns were powerful but they required as many as a dozen men to aim them, load them with ammunition, and fire them. Some of these guns were so forceful that they could shoot ammunition over an 80-mile distance. Most of the soldiers killed during the war were killed by the fire from artillery guns.

FLAME THROWERS

The German army used flame throwers to attack the Allied Powers' troops in their trenches. The flames would force them out of the trenches making them more vulnerable to attack.

GERMAN SOLDIER WITH
FLAME-THROWER

CHEMICAL WEAPON IN BARRELS

CHEMICAL WEAPONS

Chemical weapons were a deadly innovation used in World War I. Germany poisoned Allied troops with chlorine gas. Mustard gas, which was even more dangerous, was created and used by both sides of the conflict.

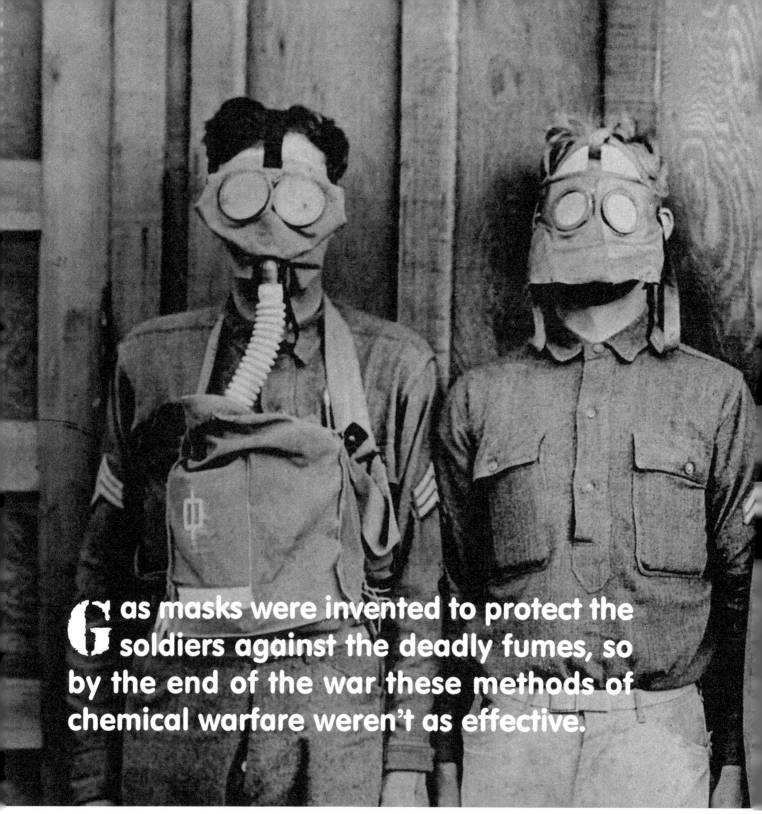

Gas masks were invented to protect the soldiers against the deadly fumes, so by the end of the war these methods of chemical warfare weren't as effective.

SOLDIERS WEARING WWI GAS MASKS.

Now you know more about the way World War I changed modern warfare. You can find more Military books from Baby Professor by searching the website of your favorite book retailer.

CPSIA information can be obtained
at www.ICGtesting.com
Printed in the USA
BVHW01s0230181018
530547BV00006B/305/P